The Pilgrims at Plymouth

LABRADOR

NEW SCOTLAND

NEWENGLAND

Plimoth

Landmark Books® Grades 2 and Up

Meet Abraham Lincoln

Meet Benjamin Franklin

Meet Christopher Columbus

Meet George Washington

Meet Thomas Jefferson

Illustrated

Liberty! How the Revolutionary War Began

The Pilgrims at Plymouth

Westward Ho! The Story of the Pioneers

The Pilgrims at Plymouth

Lucille Recht Penner ❋ **Illustrated by S. D. Schindler**

Landmark Books®

Random House 🏠 New York

To Roberta Barg

With special thanks to Carolyn Freeman Travers,
Director of Research, Plimoth Plantation

First Landmark Books® edition, 2002.

Text copyright © 1996 by Lucille Recht Penner.
Illustrations copyright © 1996 by S. D. Schindler.
All rights reserved under International and Pan-American Copyright Conventions.
Published in the United States by Random House, Inc., New York, and
simultaneously in Canada by Random House of Canada Limited, Toronto.

Originally published in slightly different form by Random House, Inc., in 1996.

Cover art courtesy of Burstein Collection/CORBIS.

www.randomhouse.com/kids

Library of Congress Cataloging-in-Publication Data
Penner, Lucille Recht.
The Pilgrims at Plymouth / by Lucille Recht Penner ; illustrations by Steven Schindler.
p.   cm. — (Landmark Books)   Includes index.
ISBN 0-375-82198-8   1. Pilgrims (New Plymouth Colony)—Juvenile literature.
2. Massachusetts—History—New Plymouth, 1620–1691—Juvenile literature.
I. Schindler, S. D., ill.   II. Title.   III. Series.   F68.P39 1996   974.4'02—dc20   95-18440

Printed in the United States of America   July 2002   10 9 8 7 6 5 4 3 2 1

RANDOM HOUSE and colophon and LANDMARK BOOKS and colophon are registered
trademarks of Random House, Inc.

Contents

"Hoist the Topsail!"

"Hoist the topsail!"

On September 6, 1620, a small wooden ship called the *Mayflower* prepared to leave Plymouth, England, and sail across the Atlantic Ocean.

Sailors scrambled up the ropes, shouted to one another, and pulled the heavy anchor on board.

Pilgrims crowded the slippery deck. They were laughing, crying, and waving good-bye to their friends and relatives.

Some of the passengers were leaving their children and parents behind. They might never see them again.

They were going to a strange, new land—America.

Christopher Columbus had discovered America more than a hundred years before, but hardly any English people had ever been there. The passengers were worried and frightened.

They knew that America was a wild land. The people who

Eighteen-year-old Priscilla Mullins was one of the Pilgrims. Her father, mother, and brother all died soon after landing in America. Priscilla married in 1622. She had eleven children.

William Bradford and his wife, Dorothy, left their five-year-old son in England with friends. William wrote a famous book about the adventures of the Pilgrims called *Of Plimoth Plantation*.

lived there—whom the English called Indians—might be their enemies. The Indians might try to kill them.

Why were they going?

Some people were leaving because they weren't safe in England. These people called themselves "Saints." They were in trouble with the king of England.

The king and most English people belonged to the Church of England. The Saints wanted to worship differently—in their own church.

But the king said no. He sent spies after the Saints. If the spies caught them holding prayer meetings, they were sent to jail. Some were even hanged.

The other passengers—whom the Saints called "Strangers"—were going to America to try to build a better life for themselves and their children.

They all crowded to the rail of the ship and called to their friends and families, "Good-bye. God bless you. We'll send for you as soon as we can."

Then the captain shouted, "Cast off!" The *Mayflower* started out across the wide, deep ocean.

Edward Winslow is the only Pilgrim whose portrait still exists.

One Hundred and Twenty-six Pairs of Shoes

What would the Pilgrims need in their new home?

Everything!

They were going to a wilderness. There would be no houses, no stores, and no friends to welcome them.

They needed to bring food to eat on the long voyage, and more food to eat while they were planting their first crops and waiting for them to grow.

They had to bring enough seeds, clothes, books, weapons, dishes, pots, pans, hoes, rakes, furniture, and tools to last for at least a year.

One passenger—William Mullins—brought 126 pairs of shoes and 13 pairs of boots! But they weren't just for him—the Pilgrims would share them.

Everyone brought chests full of clothes and linens. Beds, chairs, and tables were stacked in the ship's hold.

Most of the men brought armor to wear in case they needed to fight the Indians. They also brought muskets and gunpowder.

Sacks of cabbages, turnips, dried peas, and flour were stored in every dry corner of the ship.

Most sailors didn't worry about shoes. They went barefoot even in cold, wet weather.

The Pilgrims didn't know if they would be able to get animal hides to make leather. So they brought along plenty of shoes.

The Pilgrims wore colorful clothes. Red-brown, blue, green, and purple were their favorites.

The Indians were eager to trade for iron knives, kettles, and hoes. These were things that they didn't yet know how to make themselves.

Barrels of salted meat and smoked fish and big rounds of cheese had been rolled up the gangplank.

Farm animals were kept in small boats lashed to the deck. The *Mayflower* was noisy with the squawking of chickens, the grunting of pigs, and the bleating of goats. The Pilgrims had even brought along two dogs.

Every inch of space on the *Mayflower* was crammed with the supplies and mementos its passengers were bringing from their old homes in England.

The little ship also held the seeds of the future—the people whose dreams, courage, and hard work would create a new home and a new country far across the vast ocean.

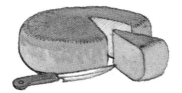

The Pilgrims had no refrigerators. They were used to eating cheese with a little green mold on top.

The *Mayflower*

The *Mayflower* was probably named after the pretty white flower of the hawthorn tree. The tree blooms in May.

What was it like to sail across the vast and mysterious Atlantic Ocean in a little wooden ship?

The *Mayflower* was only ninety feet long. That's four feet *shorter* than a basketball court! One hundred and two passengers, thirty seamen, and all their belongings were crowded into this little space.

The captain of the *Mayflower*, Master Christopher Jones, had his own cabin. The ship's officers shared one. The sailors simply wrapped themselves in a piece of old sailcloth and slept in any handy spot.

Most of the passengers lived and slept belowdecks. They spread blankets or lumpy mattresses on the floor and piled their belongings next to them.

There was hardly any room to move when everyone was

The Pilgrims had some unwanted company on the *Mayflower*—cockroaches and rats ran all over the ship.

packed in. The ceiling was less than five feet high. Most adults had to walk stooped over.

And it was hard to see in the crowded quarters. There were no lights. It was too dangerous to use candles. The wooden ship might catch fire. During the day a little light drifted in through cracks in the ceiling. At night it was black.

The ship smelled of unwashed bodies and unwashed clothes. Hardly anyone changed clothes even once during the long voyage! The men trimmed their beards, and the women braided their hair. They kept themselves neat, but it was impossible to keep clean.

In stormy weather, big waves rolled the ship from side to side. People rolled too. A lot of them were seasick.

The wind roared along the deck, and icy rain poured through every crack onto the huddled passengers. It was a cold, wet, terrifying trip.

But Master Jones and his crew worked hard to keep the ship moving steadily. Slowly the little *Mayflower* crossed the huge, empty ocean and sailed toward the American shore.

A Sailor's Life

Who were the sailors on the *Mayflower*?

We know the names of almost all the passengers. But we know hardly anything about the crew.

Master Christopher Jones commanded about thirty sailors. They had to work very hard. Two sailors stood watch on deck for four hours at a time, even in pouring rain and howling wind.

Other sailors were lookouts. They climbed high in the rigging—the web of ropes that were used to pull the sails up and down. The lookouts watched for other ships, rocks, and land. Each time the wind changed, the sails needed to be adjusted. The lookouts shouted instructions to their mates.

The man who steered the ship couldn't see where it was going. An officer on the deck above shouted orders down to him.

Seamen figured out a ship's speed by throwing a piece of wood overboard and seeing how long it took the ship to pass it.

In stormy weather it was hard for one man to move the tiller to steer the ship. Sometimes several sailors had to help turn the *Mayflower* against the strong winds and pounding waves.

Some of the sailors worked day and night repairing damage. The *Mayflower* often sprang leaks along its seams. These had to be painted with hot pitch or tar to seal them against air and water.

Sailors didn't receive much pay. But they were working for more than pay. They were working for their lives. If the *Mayflower* wasn't kept in good shape, everyone aboard would drown.

The men worked long hours. They were often wet, cold, and tired. But they did their job well and brought the *Mayflower* through fierce storms to a safe harbor on the coast of America.

Sailors couldn't be afraid of heights. They often had to climb high in the ship's rigging.

Man Overboard!

Only one passenger died on the voyage. His name was William Butten. William was buried at sea.

Ships did not carry lifeboats in the Pilgrims' time. No one was expected to survive a shipwreck far at sea. But the Pilgrims brought along a boat called a shallop—to use for exploring and fishing near shore.

For sixty-six days, the Pilgrims lived in a world of waves and sky. Few of them knew anything about the sea. They were at the mercy of Master Jones and his crew.

Master Jones was kind to the Pilgrims, but the sailors often made fun of them.

One strong, young sailor kept yelling at the seasick passengers. He said they would probably die before the trip was over—and that then he would throw their bodies overboard and take all their belongings.

One day the young sailor himself suddenly became very sick and died. He was the first person to be thrown overboard and buried at sea! The other sailors were astonished. They treated the Pilgrims more kindly after the death of their friend.

When the *Mayflower* was almost halfway across the ocean, a huge storm blew up. Heavy waves pounded the sides of the ship.

Suddenly there was a terrifying burst of noise. One of the main beams had cracked.

No one was sure what to do. Would the ship sink? Should they turn around and head back to England?

Luckily, the Pilgrims had brought along a huge iron screw to use for house-building. With it, the sailors were able to fasten the beam in place. The *Mayflower* sailed on through the stormy waters.

One day a young Pilgrim named John Howland came up on deck. The ship lurched suddenly, and he was thrown overboard. He caught hold of the rope that was trailing in the water and hung on even though the current dragged him under.

Quickly the sailors hauled up the rope. John was still clinging to it. They pulled him on board with a boathook. John Howland was saved!

A few days after this incident, Elizabeth Hopkins, the wife of Stephen Hopkins, gave birth to a son. They named him Oceanus. To the tired passengers, the birth of a baby seemed a hopeful sign of good things to come.

There were no bathrooms on the *Mayflower*. When people needed one, they used a bucket. Then it was emptied overboard.

Land Ho!

The Pilgrims' muskets were five feet long. Black gunpowder was poured into the muzzle. Then a lead ball was jammed in. When the musket was fired, flame and smoke poured out. The noise was deafening.

Early one day a long dark line appeared far on the horizon. *Land!* The Pilgrims rushed to the rail and stared through the gray morning light. They fell on their knees and thanked God.

Soon they were sailing into the calm waters of a large, safe harbor. The anchor was thrown overboard. After the long, hard voyage the Pilgrims had finally arrived in America.

But almost at once the settlers began to quarrel. Some of the Strangers said that when they got ashore they would go off by themselves.

The Pilgrim leaders were worried. They knew that their small group had to stay together. Then they could defend themselves against the Indians if they had to.

All the men held a meeting. They drew up a document called

the Mayflower Compact. It said that they would create their own government and make fair and equal laws.

Almost all the men signed the Mayflower Compact. No women signed it. In those days, women were spoken for by their husbands or fathers.

The men elected John Carver as their governor. This was the first time British colonists had ever chosen their own leader, anywhere in the British Empire.

The Pilgrims had solved one important problem. But they still had to choose a place to build their homes before the winter storms came. It was already November. There was no time to lose.

Some volunteers got ready to go exploring. They all wore armor and carried muskets and swords. Captain Miles Standish—the only soldier—was in charge.

The men said good-bye to their families and friends, rowed to shore in a small boat, and marched off down the long beach.

The women went ashore under armed guard to do the wash. They soaked great piles of dirty clothes, beat them on stones, rinsed them, and spread them on bushes to dry. While the women worked, the children and dogs ran up and down the beach.

Every day the Pilgrims who stayed on the *Mayflower* saw big whales playing nearby. A Pilgrim tried to shoot one, but the musket blew up in his face, and the whale "gave a snuff and away."

13

Handfuls of Corn

The Pilgrims came upon some round Indian houses made out of young trees tied together and covered with mats. Inside were wooden dishes, clay pots, and baskets with pretty black-and-white designs. Deers' feet, antlers, and eagle claws hung on the walls.

There was food too—parched acorns, bits of fish and deer meat, and even a piece of boiled herring! The Indians must have left their dinner and run away when they heard the Pilgrims coming.

Muskets at the ready, the Pilgrim explorers walked along the sandy white beach. On one side was the gray ocean. On the other side the dark forest loomed.

Suddenly they stopped and stared. A group of strange men and a dog were coming toward them.

Indians!

The Indians stared too. Then they turned and raced into the forest. They whistled for their dog, which—after stopping to look at the Pilgrims—followed them.

The Pilgrims dashed after them, but the Indians were faster. Soon they had disappeared. The Pilgrims lost their way among the dark trees. Thorny bushes tore at their clothes and scratched their armor. They were hungry and thirsty.

Finally they came upon a spring of fresh water. It was delicious. The Pilgrims drank and drank.

When they felt better, they walked on. They came to a hill covered with little heaps of sand. The Pilgrims dug into one of the heaps and found a big basket filled with Indian seed corn.

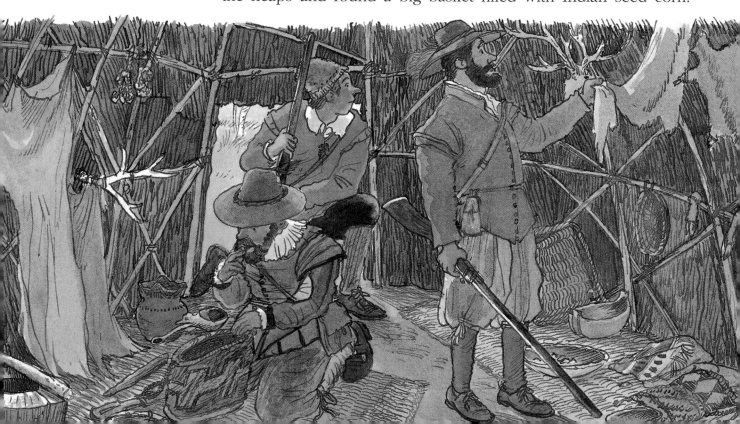

They stuffed handfuls into their pockets. They poured more corn into an old iron kettle they found nearby, which must have been left by earlier explorers.

But when the Pilgrims dug into some other heaps, they found skeletons. They had stumbled onto an Indian graveyard. Carefully they covered the graves they had disturbed.

On their way back to the *Mayflower*, the Pilgrims saw a small tree that had been bent over and tied to the ground. Under the tree was a little mound of acorns.

It was strange.

William Bradford stepped closer to get a good look. Suddenly he gave a cry. A noose had closed over his foot. The tree shot up in the air and he was dangling upside down. He had stepped in an Indian deer trap!

The men cut him down and returned to the ship. They had walked for many miles. But still they had not found a place to build their new homes. They would have to go exploring again.

Wild Beasts and Wild Men

Eighteen men set off in the shallop.

The wind blew hard, and huge waves splashed them with cold, salty water. The men shivered. Water froze and formed crusts of ice on their clothes.

As they sailed along the shore, they saw a group of Indians bent over a big black object on the beach.

The Pilgrims decided to land. But by the time they reached shore, the Indians had run away. The black object was still lying on the sand. It looked like the biggest fish the Pilgrims had ever seen.

The light was fading fast. So the Pilgrims made a campfire, piled up a barricade of branches, and went to sleep. They would take turns standing guard.

In the middle of the night, they were awakened by a wild shriek: "Woath woach ha ha hach woach!"

The guard shouted, "Arm! Arm!" and the men raced for their muskets. They quickly fired off a volley.

The shrieking stopped.

The Pilgrims were very frightened. One of the sailors told them he was sure it was only a wild beast howling. He had heard the same noise in Greenland. In the morning they heard the horrible shriek again. Suddenly the guard shouted, "Men! Indians! Men!"

Arrows began to fly. Indians came running. The Pilgrims grabbed their muskets and fired.

One big Indian stood behind a nearby tree and shot arrows at the Pilgrims. One of the men took careful aim and hit the tree. The Indian was showered with bark and leaves. He gave a horrible yell and ran away. The other Indians raced after him.

None of the Pilgrims were hurt, but several coats that had been hung on nearby branches while the men slept had been shot full of arrows!

The Pilgrims climbed back into the shallop and sailed on. But they were in for more trouble.

Soon a bad storm blew up. The shallop's rudder broke, and the men had to steer with oars. Then, as they pulled for shore, the mast cracked! The sail fell into the sea. The men were afraid they would all be drowned, but they managed to pull themselves onto a small island.

For days the Pilgrims rested, prayed, and dried their wet clothes and muskets. The island wasn't big enough for a settlement, but they decided to explore the quiet harbor nearby. Later, they were to name it Plymouth.

While the men were out exploring, ten-year-old Francis Billington made firecrackers—with gunpowder—and set them off in his father's cabin. Then he fired a musket.

There was an open barrel of gunpowder nearby, and it was only by great good luck that no one was hurt or the ship blown up.

A New Home

The blue waters of Plymouth Harbor sparkled in bright sunlight. Beyond the beach grew a tall, green forest. Ducks, herons, swans, and geese nested along the shore. Flounder and cod swam in the cold ocean current. The sandy bottom was home for all kinds of shellfish.

The Pilgrims pulled the shallop ashore and went exploring. They found a brook. In England, people didn't drink much water. They dumped their garbage into the rivers and streams. The water tasted terrible. But here the water was sweet and clear.

Strawberries, raspberries, herbs, watercress, leeks, and onions grew nearby. The forest was full of pine, walnut, birch, ash, beech, and sassafras trees.

The Pilgrims used a long piece of knotted rope with a lead weight on the end to measure the depth of Plymouth Harbor. They let out the rope slowly and counted the knots as they disappeared under the water. The harbor was deep enough for large sailing ships to ride at anchor.

18

It would be wonderful to have so much wood available. But big trees were hard to cut down. It took a long time to fell even one tree with an ax.

That is why the Pilgrims were happy to find that fields for planting had already been cleared by the Indians, although there was no sign that Indians lived anywhere nearby.

From the top of a high hill, the men could look over the surrounding countryside and far out to sea. Miles Standish said that this would be a good place to put cannons. It would be easy to defend this spot.

Plymouth wasn't perfect. The Pilgrims would have liked to start their colony where a river ran into the sea. They wanted to be able to sail inland to hunt, and to trade with the Indians.

But time was running out.

They returned to the *Mayflower*. We have good news, they told their friends. We have found our new home.

The Pilgrims were pleased to have a supply of sassafras trees close by. Sassafras bark was boiled and made into a popular medicine. It was supposed to be good for almost every illness.

Captain Standish shot an eagle. The Pilgrims ate it and said that it tasted like mutton.

Francis Billington, the boy who had set off the fire-crackers, climbed a very high tree. He thought he saw a big sea in the distance. He and one of the sailors went to look. The "sea" turned out to be two lakes. They were later named Billington's Sea.

Hard Times

What could the Pilgrims do for shelter against the rain, the wind, and the cold while they built their houses? Already many of them were weak and sick.

They begged Master Jones to anchor the *Mayflower* in Plymouth Harbor until the first houses were finished. But the sailors were anxious to return to England. Some of them wanted to put the Pilgrims and their belongings on shore at once and sail home. But Master Jones was a good friend to the Pilgrims. He agreed to stay.

This meant that the women and children could remain on the ship with their belongings. And the men had a dry place to return to each night to sleep.

One day a Pilgrim who was hoping to shoot a duck hid in the reeds and saw twelve Indian warriors marching toward Plymouth. He hurried back to give the warning. At the edge of the woods he met two Pilgrims chopping trees. They dropped their tools and ran to get their muskets. The Indians didn't attack. But when the men went back for their tools, they were gone. The Indians had taken them.

One day John Goodman went for a walk with his spaniel. Suddenly two wolves leaped out and tried to grab the little dog. It ran to Goodman. He picked up a stick and threw it at one of the wolves. They ran back into the forest. The wolves were probably as hungry as the Pilgrims. That was why they were so bold.

But even with the *Mayflower* for shelter, the Pilgrims suffered a terrible winter. They couldn't plant their crops until the frozen ground thawed. And they did not know how to live off the land. Most wild fruits had already shriveled in the cold. Sometimes they found nuts and acorns, but never enough to fill their stomachs.

The ocean and brooks teemed with fish, but they hadn't brought the right sort of hooks to catch them.

There were animals in the woods, but the Pilgrims didn't know how to make deer traps like the one that had "caught" William Bradford. Their muskets were clumsy to aim and tremendously loud. After a shot was fired, all the animals ran away.

So the Pilgrims tightened their belts, worked hard, shivered with cold, and looked forward to the warmth and plenty of spring.

Raising the Rafters

The weather got worse and worse.

It rained and blew so hard that the Pilgrims couldn't even sail the shallop to shore. In fact, Master Jones had to have two extra anchors thrown overboard to keep the *Mayflower* itself from blowing away!

A work party finally landed on December 23 and began the construction of the common house—a building that would be shared by all. The weather stayed so bad it took twenty-three days to build. Next, they laid out a street. Its name was simply "the Street." There wasn't any other street to confuse it with.

The street led from the beach to a steep hill. At the top, the Pilgrims built a wooden platform for their heavy cannons.

Then lots were laid out along the street. They were very narrow. The Pilgrims didn't have the energy or the materials to build big houses. One-room houses would have to do.

Single men and servants had to live with families. That way, there would be fewer houses to build.

One by one, the little houses began to rise. Each one had a big fireplace for cooking. A chimney carried most of the smoke outside—and also most of the heat. These little houses weren't very warm.

The houses were dark too. They had small windows, and in place of glass the Pilgrims used cloth rubbed with oil. Floors were packed-down dirt, scattered with a carpet of rushes.

A ladder led to a loft where food was stored in sacks and barrels. More food—if the harvest was successful—would be kept in two storehouses that the Pilgrims built near their common house. They planned to store their food together and share all they had.

The Pilgrims were beginning to carve a real town from the wilderness.

To make boards, the Pilgrims dug a pit about six feet deep. They laid a huge log across the pit. Then one man jumped in, another stood above him, and together they sawed the log into boards.

The Pilgrims didn't build log cabins. Oak posts and logs were used to make the frame of each house. Then clapboard was nailed over the frames. Pilgrim boys made big wooden pegs called trunnels to fasten the posts together.

Layers of thatch made from coarse grass or reeds made a roof that lasted for many years. But repairs were often needed. Birds and insects damaged the thatch. Wind and rain battered it. And sometimes a spark from the chimney caused a fire, and the whole roof burst into flames.

The Great Sickness

A page from William Bradford's diary.

During their first terrible winter in America, more than half the Pilgrims died.

It was damp and cold on the *Mayflower*. On shore it was worse. The men who were working to build houses were often soaked with rain. Once their clothes got wet, they rarely had a chance to dry out. Many people coughed and shook with fever.

It was frightening. Sometimes two or three people died in one day. People became ill so quickly that they fell down right in the fields. They had to be carried to the common house.

The little building was soon packed with sick people. They lay elbow to elbow. So many were sick that the healthy ones could hardly take care of them.

But they tried. As William Bradford wrote, friends and families "spared no pains night nor day, but with abundance of toil and hazard of their own health, fetched them wood, made them fires, dressed their meat, made their beds, washed their loathsome clothes, clothed and unclothed them. In a word, did all the homely and necessary offices for them which dainty and queasy stomachs cannot endure to hear named...."

One morning, the people on the *Mayflower* saw flames shooting up into the sky. They were horrified. Had the Indians attacked, killed their friends, and set fire to the common house? They found their friends cold and frightened, but safe. A spark had blown onto the thatched roof of the common house and set it on fire. The sick people had had to flee into the freezing morning.

No one was hurt, but it had been a close escape. Loaded muskets were stored in the common house. There could have been a terrible explosion.

Four-year-old Mary Allerton lost her mother during the first hard winter at Plymouth. Mary lived to be eighty-seven. When she died in 1704, she was the only survivor of the original settlers.

Only five of the eighteen women who had sailed on the *Mayflower* survived the first winter.

Twenty-nine unmarried men, hired hands, and servants had made the trip. Nineteen of them died. So did half the married men.

But almost all the children lived. All seven of the girls and ten of the thirteen boys survived. Perhaps their parents gave them their own warm clothing and choice bits of food.

The Pilgrims buried their dead secretly, at night. They were afraid that the Indians would attack if they knew how few of the Pilgrims were left alive.

Often the Pilgrims saw Indian campfires in the distance. All during that winter, no Indians came close. But the Pilgrims kept worrying. What would happen when they and the Indians finally met?

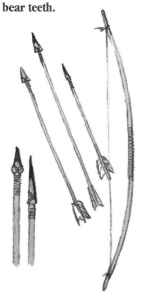

All the Indians carried bows and arrows. Some of the arrow points were made of eagle claws, others of bear teeth.

Welcome!

One day an Indian walked straight into Plymouth. He strolled right up the street to the common house. The astonished Pilgrims ran out.

"Welcome!" the Indian said.

He spoke English!

The Pilgrims stared at him. The Indian carried a bow and two arrows. He was "stark naked, only a leather about his waist." This embarrassed the Pilgrims. They lent him a long red coat to wear.

His name was Samoset, he said. He explained that he had learned some English words from English fishermen. He was from the north. The Indians who had lived at Plymouth—the Patuxet

The Indians made beautiful designs on their clothing with paint, beads, and porcupine quills.

Indians—had almost all been killed a few years ago by a terrible plague.

The Pilgrims thought this was sad. But they were also glad "there would be none to hinder their possession of this place."

When Samoset left, the Pilgrims gave him a knife, a ring, and a bracelet. Samoset liked the presents. The next day, he returned with five tall Indians carrying beaver skins to trade to the Pilgrims.

Soon he came again with an Indian named Squanto. Squanto spoke even better English than Samoset. He told the Pilgrims that he had actually been to England!

Before the Pilgrims could ask Squanto how this had happened, they looked up and saw an astonishing sight. A warrior chief was standing on a hill across the river. Behind him were sixty brightly painted Indians.

Many of the Indians wore only a leather band around their waists, with strips of leather hanging down in front. They dressed to move easily through the forest.

When Edward Winslow crossed the river to talk to Massasoit, he wore a full suit of armor and carried his sword. The chief liked these things very much and offered to buy them.

Chief Yellow Feather

Massasoit's necklace was made of white bird or fish bone beads. He also wore a knife and a tobacco pouch around his neck.

Was this a war party?

The Pilgrims were outnumbered. They had only twenty men strong enough to fight if they needed to.

What should they do? The Pilgrims quickly gathered up food and presents. Then Edward Winslow took the gifts and splashed across the brook.

He bowed to the warrior chief, whose name was Massasoit, or Ousamequin—which means Yellow Feather—and gave him a chain with a jewel in it, as well as a pair of knives, some butter, and a pot of brandy.

Then Edward told Chief Massasoit that King James of England saluted him in words of love and peace and hoped he would be his friend. Also, Edward said, the governor of Plymouth Colony wanted to meet him, trade with him, and make peace with him.

Of course, Edward Winslow and Massasoit didn't speak the same language. Squanto was their interpreter. Without him, they couldn't have talked at all!

Massasoit agreed to come to Plymouth and meet Governor Carver if Edward Winslow stayed behind as hostage. Twenty Indians put down their bows and arrows and followed the chief across the brook.

Captain Miles Standish met them on the shore. A group of men carrying muskets stood behind him. They escorted Massasoit to a half-finished house up the street. Inside, the Pilgrims had placed a green rug and a mound of cushions. As soon as Massasoit sat down there was a roll of drums and a trumpet fanfare. Then Governor Carver was escorted in.

The governor and the chief kissed each other's hands. They ate and drank together. Then they arranged a treaty. The Pilgrims agreed to live in peace with Massasoit's people, the Wampanoags. When they came to visit each other, they would always come unarmed. Any Wampanoag or Pilgrim who harmed a member of the other group would be punished. And if any outsiders attacked either the Wampanoags or the Pilgrims, they would come to each other's defense.

This was a wonderful treaty. The friendship between the Pilgrims and the Indians lasted for more than fifty years.

One of the Pilgrims blew a trumpet when Governor Carver appeared. Later, the Indians took turns trying to blow it.

Skulls and Bones

Every day, more and more Indians came to visit Plymouth. Men brought their wives and children. And all of them were hungry!

The Pilgrims didn't know what to do. If they fed everyone who dropped in, they wouldn't have any food left. But not to offer food to their guests would be rude.

The Pilgrims decided to send Edward Winslow and Stephen Hopkins to talk to Massasoit. They would ask him to stop his people from visiting so often. Squanto would go along as interpreter.

The men walked for three days. They passed deserted cornfields heaped with white skulls and bones. So many people had died in the terrible plague that the Indians had not been able to bury them all.

When they arrived, Edward Winslow explained their problem. The Pilgrims, he said, were strangers in this country. They didn't have much food. Would Massasoit be kind enough to ask his people not to drop in for meals? Edward waited for an answer. He was afraid Massasoit would be angry. But Massasoit understood. He promised that his men wouldn't bother the Pilgrims anymore.

One day Governor Carver came back from working in the fields, complaining that his head hurt. In a few hours he was dead. The Pilgrims saluted him with "volleys of shot by all that bore arms."

William Bradford was elected the new governor of Plymouth Colony. He was re-elected thirty times.

On May 12, Edward Winslow, whose wife had died six weeks before, married Susanna White, widow of William White. She was the mother of Peregrine White, the first Pilgrim child born in the New World.

In some of the Indian towns where Edward and Stephen stopped, they were given roasted crabs to eat. The crabs were cooked right in the hot coals of the fire.

Then he invited the Pilgrim messengers to spend the night in his tent.

There was only one bed, made of boards covered with mats. The Pilgrims would share it with Massasoit and his wife. They lay down, hoping to get some rest. But it was crowded and noisy. Winslow wrote, "The Indians sang themselves to sleep." The Pilgrims stayed awake all night.

They were very hungry in the morning, but there was no breakfast. At lunchtime one of the Indians shot two big fish with arrows. These were cooked over a fire and tasted very good. Forty people shared them!

Before the Pilgrims left, Massasoit said he wanted to help them. He would arrange for Squanto to travel to the nearby tribes and collect furs for the Pilgrims.

Edward Winslow thanked him with all his heart. It was good news to bring home to Plymouth.

Edward assured Massasoit that his special messengers would always be welcome at Plymouth.

How would the Pilgrims know his special friends? Edward gave Massasoit a copper chain. Whenever Massasoit wanted to send a messenger, he should give him the chain to wear. Then the Pilgrims would know that the messenger had come from Massasoit.

Squanto

One day John Billington—the brother of the boy who had set off the fireworks—got lost in the woods. He lived on berries and water until some Indians found him. They brought him home to Plymouth, wearing many strings of beads that they had given him.

Who was Squanto? Where had he come from? How had he learned English?

Squanto was a Patuxet Indian. He had been born right where the Pilgrims built their town. But before the Pilgrims sailed on the *Mayflower*, Squanto had been kidnapped by an English sea captain.

After several years in England and Spain, he managed to return home. But when he got to Plymouth, he found that all the Patuxets—every member of his family and all his friends—had died of plague. Nothing was left of his home but deserted fields strewn with bones.

So Squanto went to live with Massasoit and his tribe—the Wampanoags.

But after he met the Pilgrims, Squanto decided to stay with them. He lived with them at Plymouth for the rest of his life and helped them in many important ways.

He taught them to plant corn in the spring, "when the oak leaves are as big as a mouse's ear." Four or five corn seeds had to be planted together in a little hill of earth. One or two herrings were put in each hill along with the seeds. The herrings provided food for the plants as they grew.

Without this corn, the Pilgrims would have starved. The seeds they had brought from England produced hardly any grain or vegetables at all.

Squanto also taught the Pilgrims which plants and berries were safe to eat. He showed them how to tread eels out of the mud with their feet and how to spear large fish. And he was their guide when they needed to travel through the strange, dark forest to hunt or to trade with Indians.

Governor William Bradford wrote in his journal that Squanto was "a special instrument sent of God for [the Pilgrims'] good beyond their expectation."

The Indians had lots to teach the Pilgrims about fishing. They caught fish with spears, nets woven of grasses, and hooks made from animal bones.

Harvest Time

After the corn was picked, the husks were braided and hung from the rafters.

Suddenly it was autumn. Leaves were turning gold and frost coated the pumpkins in the early mornings. It was time to gather the harvest.

"God be praised," Edward Winslow wrote in his journal, "we had a good increase of Indian corn."

In fact, the Pilgrims gathered so many little ears of bright red, yellow, and blue Indian corn that each person would receive a peck—eight quarts!—of cornmeal every week.

They stored the corn in the common house along with barrels of salted fish, meat, and fowl. Dried fruit and vegetables were threaded and hung from rafters.

There were only four married Pilgrim women left alive by the time of the harvest celebration—Elizabeth Hopkins, Susanna White Winslow, Elinore Billington, and Mary Brewster. They prepared the meal. Children and servants helped.

No one would starve this winter! And the Pilgrims would eat their meals in the shelter of their own houses—not on the rolling *Mayflower*.

Governor Bradford declared a holiday—a day of rejoicing. Instead of laboring in the fields, the Pilgrims would rest, play games, and feast on the foods of their new land.

Four men went hunting. They shot wild fowl—ducks, geese, and probably turkeys. Cod, salmon, bass, eel, lobster, mussels, and clams were gathered from the sea and boiled, roasted, and baked in stews and soups. Cornmeal was cooked in pies, bread, soups, puddings, and little cakes that were like pancakes.

Massasoit was invited to share in the celebration. The Pilgrims were shocked when he brought along ninety men! How could they feed them all?

But Massasoit knew what to do. He sent some of the Indians into the forest. Soon they returned with five deer. Now there was enough food for a real feast!

The deer meat the Indians brought was probably roasted on a spit over a fire. A child turned the spit. It was hot, boring work. But the smell of the roasting meat was wonderful.

Thanksgiving

The thanksgiving feast was a joyous one. It lasted for three days!

The Pilgrims and Indians ate, drank, and showed off for each other. The Pilgrim men gave a military parade. They marched in formation to the music of drums and fired off noisy muskets. The Indians danced and shot at targets with their bows and arrows.

Everyone ran races, played games, and ate and ate and ate. When it got dark, the Pilgrims and Indians slept. In the morning they woke up and began playing and feasting all over again.

The Pilgrims counted their blessings.

Less than a year before, they had staggered onto a strange, foreign shore—after a long, exhausting ocean voyage—and stared into a dark, threatening forest. Now, where tall trees and empty fields had stood was a new town—Plymouth.

Although half the original settlers had died, the Pilgrims who remained were strong and healthy. They had managed to plant, tend crops, and gather a great harvest of corn, squash, and beans.

And they had signed a treaty of peace with the Indians. As one Pilgrim said, "We walk as peaceably and safely in the wood as on the highways of England." When the Pilgrims had first seen Massasoit and his men in their bright paint and feathers, they were terrified. Now the Pilgrims and Indians were sharing a feast.

Almost four hundred years have passed since that first joyous celebration. Today—at Thanksgiving time—we still tell and retell the story of the remarkable band of Pilgrims who left their homes and crossed the ocean to plant the seeds of a new world.

Index

LABRADOR

NEW SCOTLAND

NEWENGLAND

Plimoth